CAJUN AND ZYDECO CLASSICS ❦ FOR ACCORDION

* Arranged by Gary Meisner
~ Arranged by Peter Deneff

ISBN 978-1-5400-8284-8

Visit Hal Leonard Online at
www.halleonard.com

Contact us:
Hal Leonard
7777 West Bluemound Road
Milwaukee, WI 53213
Email: info@halleonard.com

In Europe, contact:
Hal Leonard Europe Limited
42 Wigmore Street
Marylebone, London, W1U 2RN
Email: info@halleonardeurope.com

In Australia, contact:
Hal Leonard Australia Pty. Ltd.
4 Lentara Court
Cheltenham, Victoria, 3192 Australia
Email: info@halleonard.com.au

BAYOU PON PON

Words and Music by HANK WILLIAMS
and JIMMIE DAVIS

Oh, ___ tu viens me ja - mais, petit coeur. ___ Tu mà aban-don -
Oh, ___ je tu voir ja - mais, petit coeur. ___ Tu me viens

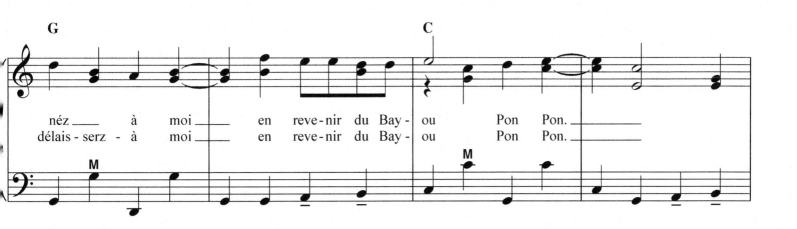

néz ___ à moi ___ en reve-nir du Bay - ou Pon Pon. ___
délais - serz - à moi ___ en reve-nir du Bay - ou Pon Pon.

Oh, _____ tu viens me ja - mais, petit coeur. ___ Tu m'à aban-don -
Oh, _____ je tu voir ja - mais, petit coeur. ___ Tu me viens

néz _____ à moi _____ en reve-nir du Bay - ou Pon Pon. _____
délais - serz - à moi _____ en reve-nir du Bay - ou Pon Pon. _____

BIG MAMOU

Words and Music by LINK DAVIS
and MACY LELA HENRY

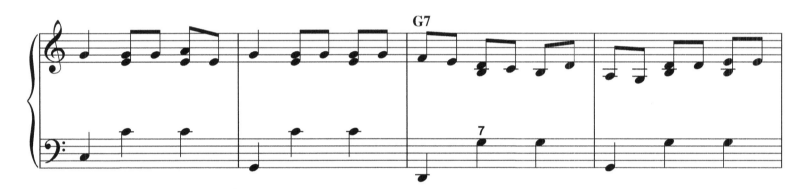

BROKEN HEARTED

Words and Music by
JOHN DELAFOSE

COLINDA

Words and Music by JIMMIE DAVIS,
DOC GUIDRY and L.J. LEBLANC

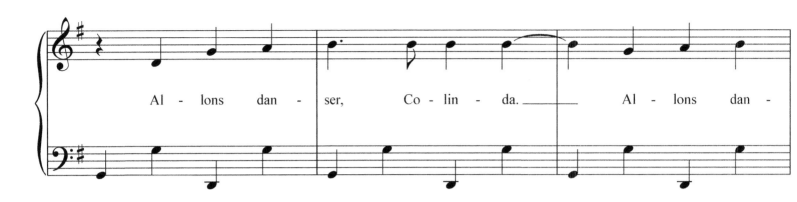

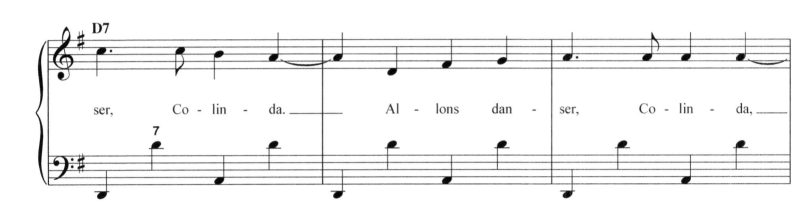

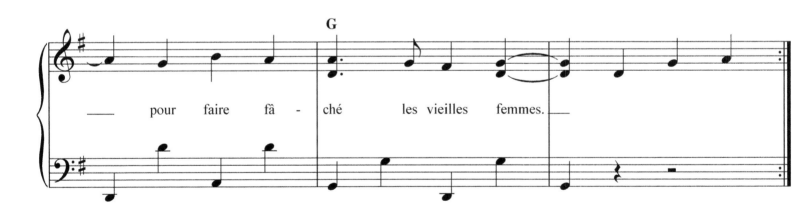

CRY TO ME

Words and Music by
BERT RUSSELL

And ba-by, you don't have to walk, ___

walk ___ all a-lone. ___ You'll see. If ___ your ___

lov-er ___ don't ___ re-turn, ___

take my hand, - { won't you, hon-ey,   come on and ___ walk with me, ___
                  { hon-ey child,   come on and ___ walk with me, _

DIGGY LIGGY LO

Words and Music by
J.D. MILLER

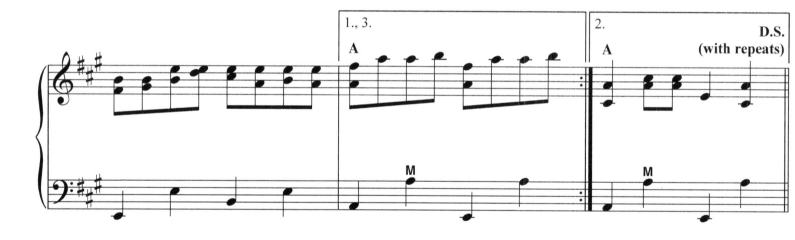

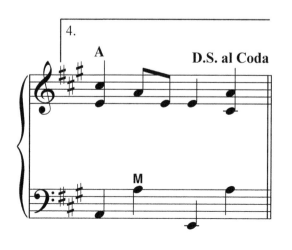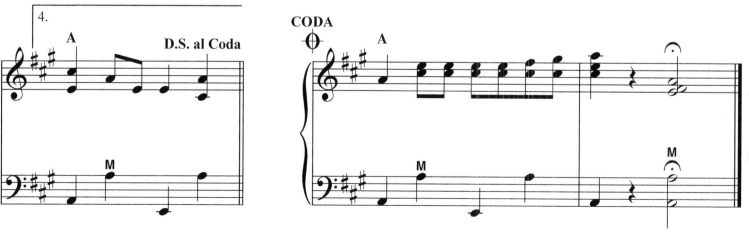

I'M COMING HOME

Words and Music by
CLIFTON CHENIER

I'm _____ I'm com-in' home, 'cause I

feel, feel so all a-lone. _____ I ___ com-in'

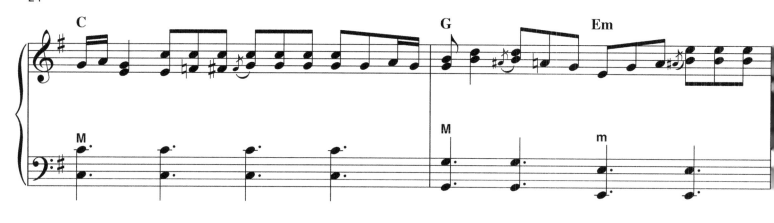

And re- | mem ber, | be- fore I get
I'm __ | | I'm com- in'

home, _____ | I'm gon-na | start, | start all | o - ver a-
home, _____ | 'cause I __ | feel, | feel so | all __ a-

IKO IKO

Words and Music by BARBARA ANN HAWKINS,
JOAN MARIE JOHNSON and ROSA LEE HAWKINS

Talk - in' 'bout hey now! Hey now!

JAMBALAYA
(On the Bayou)

Words and Music by
HANK WILLIAMS

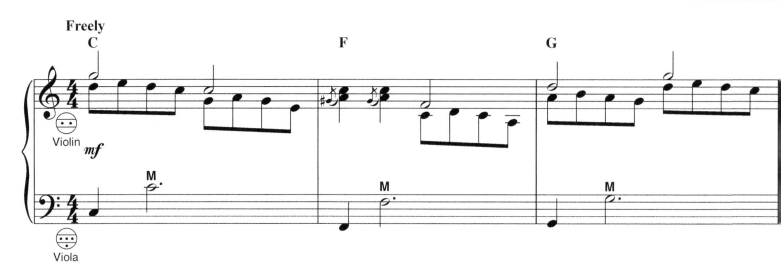

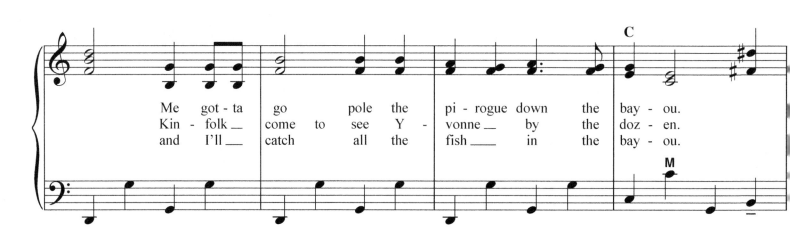

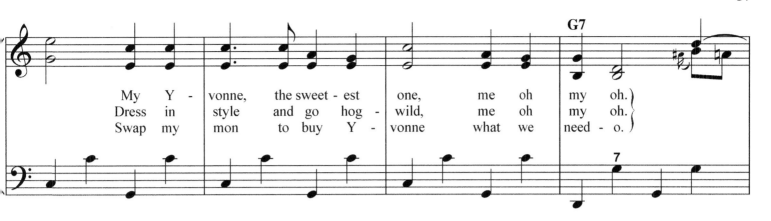

My Y - vonne, the sweet - est one, me oh my oh.
Dress in style and go hog - wild, me oh my oh.
Swap my mon to buy Y - vonne what we need - o.

Son of a gun, we'll have big fun on the bay - ou.

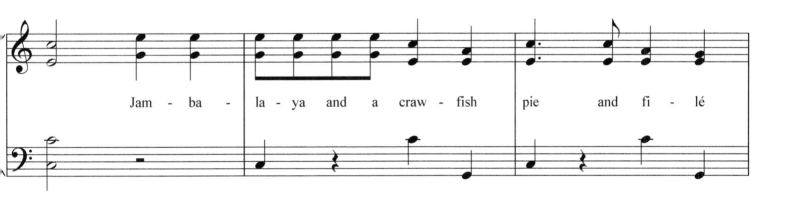

Jam - ba - la - ya and a craw - fish pie and fi - lé

gum - bo, 'cause to - night I'm gon - na see my ma cher a -

mi - o.   Pick gui - tar,   fill fruit jar   and be

gay - o.   Son of a   gun, we'll have big   fun   on the

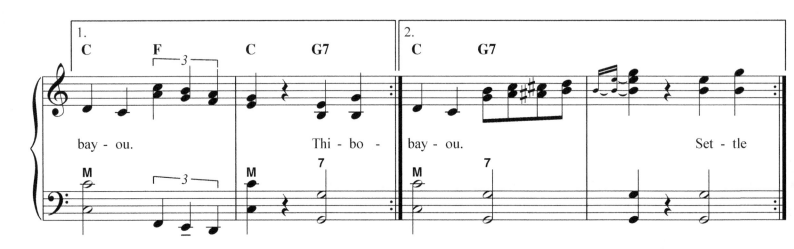

bay - ou.   Thi - bo - bay - ou.   Set - tle

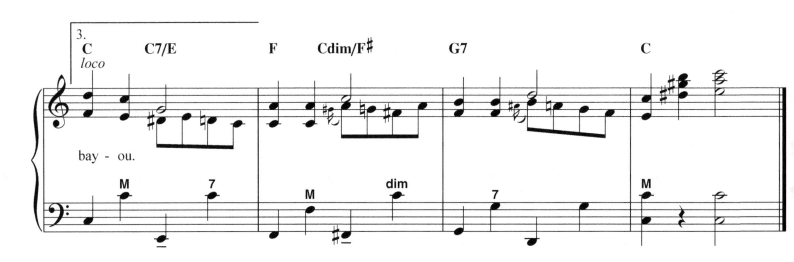

bay - ou.

MY TOOT TOOT

Words and Music by
SIDNEY SIMIEN

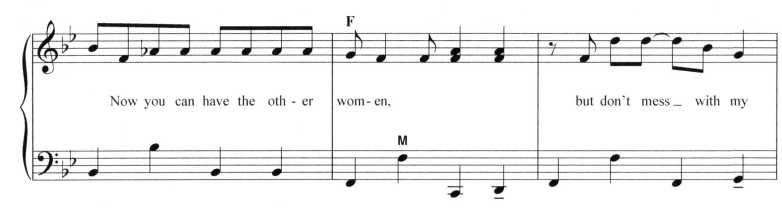

Now you can have the oth - er wom - en, but don't mess _ with my

Toot Toot.

((1., D.S.) When she was born in her birth suit,
(2.) Now she look good in her bi - ki - ni suit.

the doc - tor slapped her be - hind. _ Said you're gon - na be
A man can dream that she's fine. _ Oh, she's my all, _ she's

spe - cial, you sweet, _ lit - tle Toot _ Toot.
spe - cial, she's my heart, _ she's mine.

Now you can look as much, ____
I'm the ac - cor - di-on man ____

but if you much as touch, _
from the bay - ou land, _

you're gon - na have your-self a case.
start - ed the Toot Toot _ train. _

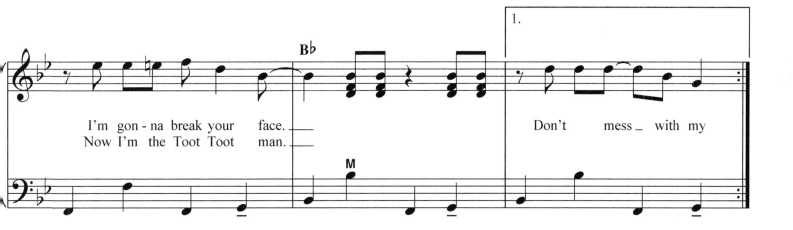

I'm gon - na break your face. ____
Now I'm the Toot Toot man. ____

1.

Don't mess _ with my

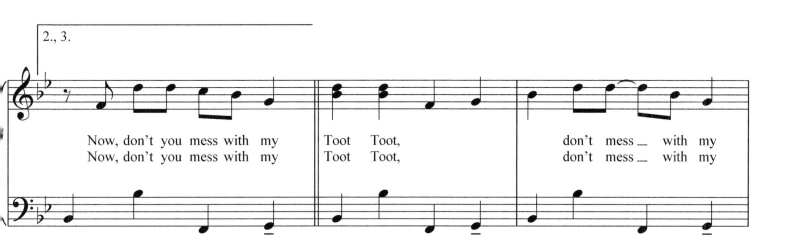

2., 3.

Now, don't you mess with my
Now, don't you mess with my

Toot Toot,
Toot Toot,

don't mess _ with my
don't mess _ with my

Toot   Toot.
Toot   Toot.

Now you can sing my   song,____
Now you can have the oth - er |wom - en,

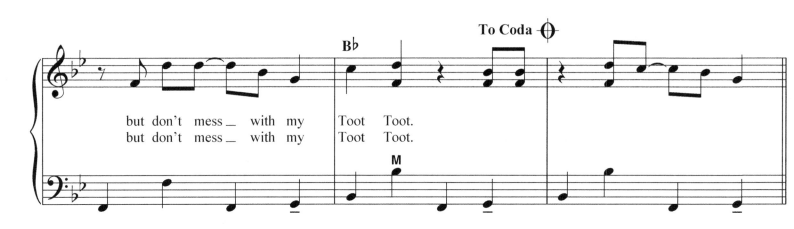

but don't mess __ with my
but don't mess __ with my

Toot   Toot.
Toot   Toot.

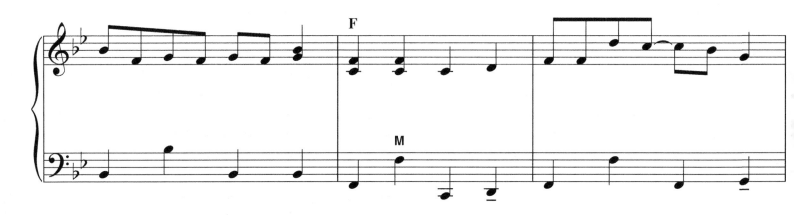

D.S. al Coda
(take 2nd ending)

Don't mess __ with my

LOUISIANA MAN

Words and Music by
DOUG KERSHAW

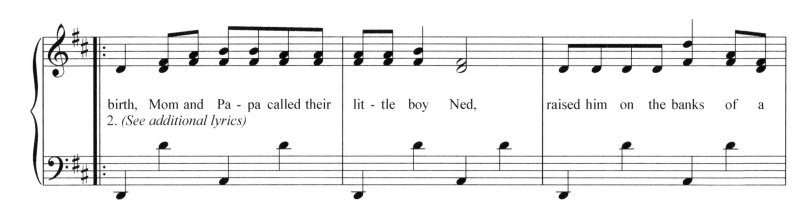

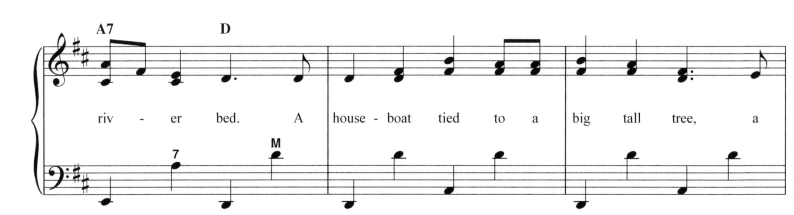

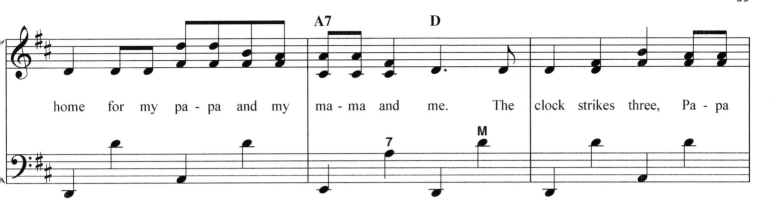

home for my pa - pa and my ma - ma and me. The clock strikes three, Pa - pa

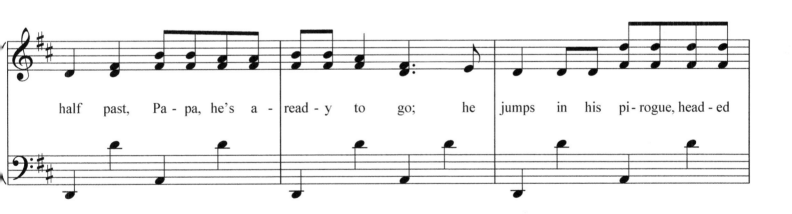

jumps to his feet, al - read - y Ma - ma's cook - ing Pa - pa some - thing to eat. At

half past, Pa - pa, he's a - read - y to go; he jumps in his pi - rogue, head - ed

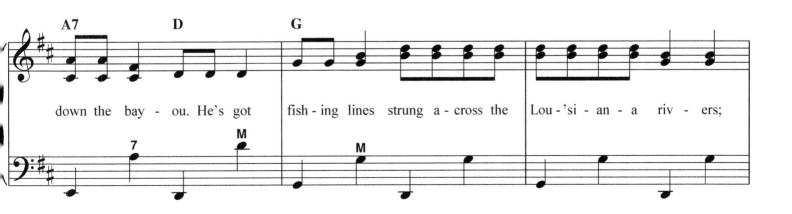

down the bay - ou. He's got fish - ing lines strung a - cross the Lou - 'si - an - a riv - ers;

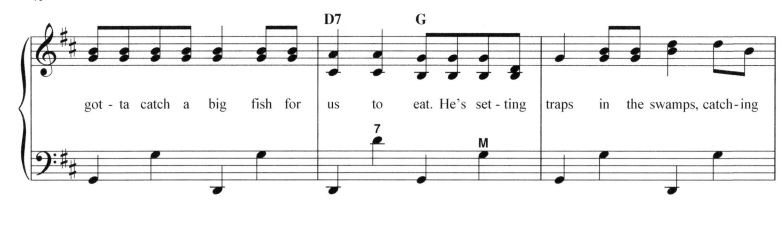

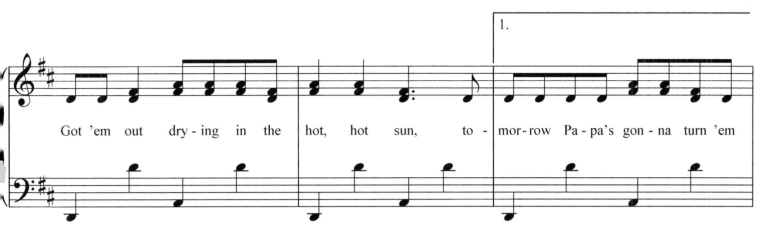

Got 'em out dry - ing in the hot, hot sun, to - mor - row Pa - pa's gon - na turn 'em

in - to mon'. They come back a - gain, first there's work to be done."

Additional Lyrics

2. They call mama Rita and my daddy Jack
   Little baby brother on the floor, that's Mack.
   Bren and Lin are the family twins
   Big brother Ed's on the bayou, fishing.

   On the river, floats papa's great big boat
   That's how papa goes into town.
   Takes every bit of a night and a day
   To even reach a place where people stay.

   I can hardly wait until tomorrow comes around
   That's the day papa takes the furs to town.
   Papa promised me, Ned and I could go
   Even let me see a cowboy show.

   I seen cowboys and Indians for the first time then
   I told my papa, "I gotta go again."
   Papa said, "Son, we got lines to run.
   We'll come back again, first there's work to be done."

MARDI GRAS MAMBO

Words and Music by FRANKIE ADAMS,
KEN ELLIOT and LOU WELSCH

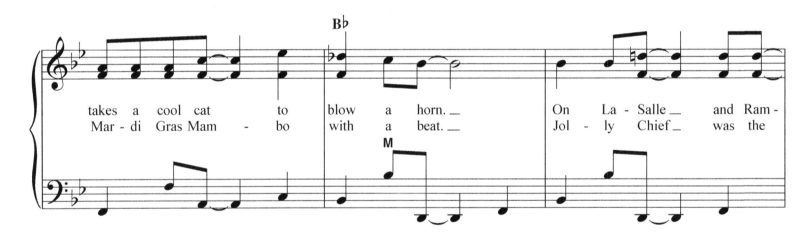

MATILDA

Words and Music by GEORGE A. KHOURY
and HUEY THIERRY

SUGAR BEE

Words and Music by
EDDIE SHULER

Sug - ar Bee, Sug - ar Bee, Sug - ar

Bee, Sug - ar Bee,   Sug - ar   Bee,   Sug - ar Bee,

Sug - ar   Bee, Sug - ar Bee,   Sug - ar Bee, Sug - ar

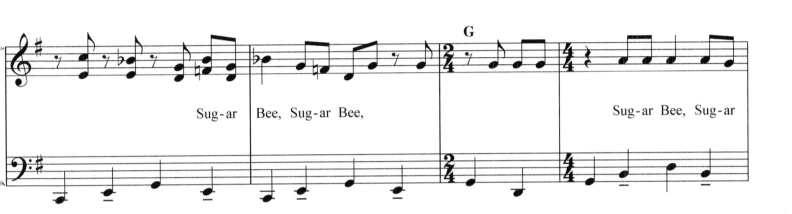

Bee,   look what __ you done to   me. __

Well,   you   said you'd be   my hon - ey   all   night   long.
              came __ home this morn - in' 'bout a   quar - ter to   four.

When I found you, ba - by, you were do - in'___ wrong.___ Sug - ar Bee, Sug - ar
Found an - oth - er wom - an sit - tin' at my ___ door. ___

Bee, Sug-ar Bee, Sug-ar Bee, Sug-ar Bee, Sug-ar

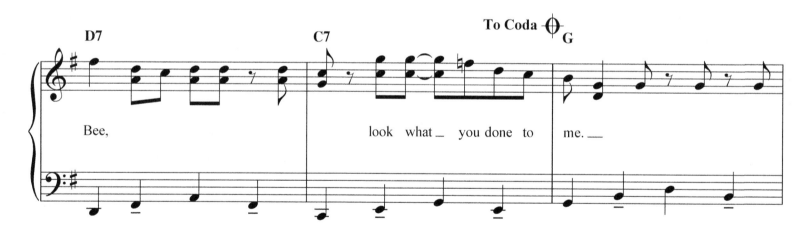

Bee, look what ___ you done to me. ___

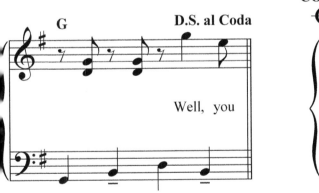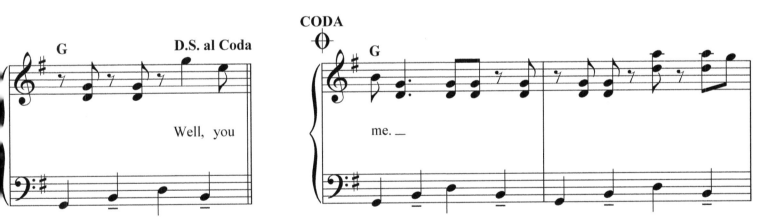

Well, you

me. —

look what — you done to me.

ZYDECO GRIS GRIS

Words and Music by
MICHAEL DOUCET

Tout par - tout au - ras __
Tout par - tout au - ras __

__ du bay - ou, mousse - là ba - lance aux gros __ chênes verts.
__ du bay - ou, Cré - oles yé tout a - pé __ chan - ter.

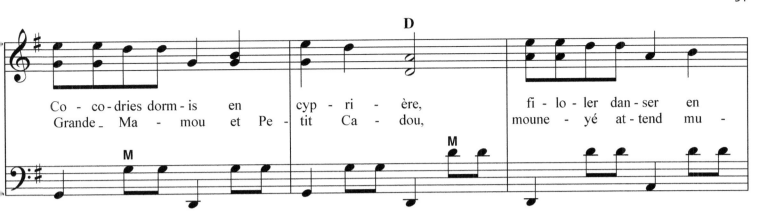

Co - co-dries dorm-is en cyp - ri - ère,
fi - lo - ler dan - ser en

Grande Ma - mou et Pe - tit Ca - dou,
moune - yé at - tend mu -

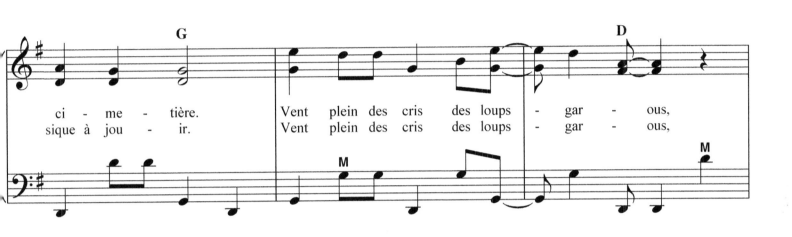

ci - me - tière.
Vent plein des cris des loups - gar - ous,

sique à jou - ir.
Vent plein des cris des loups - gar - ous,

pieds a - pé ta - pé rhyth - me - là fou.
Moune - là con - nait y'o - lé

mousse - là ba - lance aux gros chênes verts.
Co - co-dries dor - mis en cy -

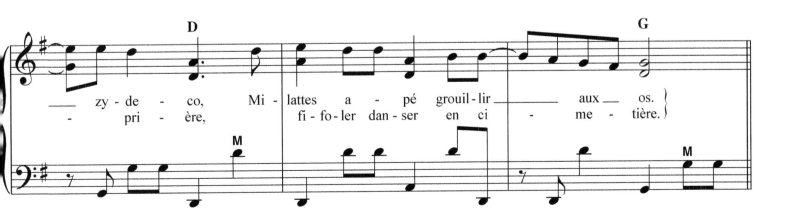

zy - de - co, Mi - lattes a - pé grouil - lir aux os.

- pri - ère, fi - fo - ler dan - ser en ci - me - tière.

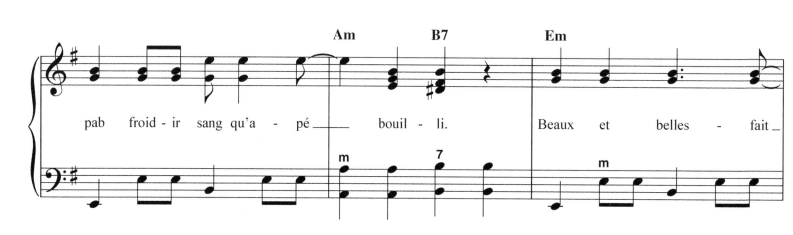

Loin, loin, cy - pri - ère noir, tout que-q'un cré - ole crie:

Zy - de - co!

THE ORIGINAL NEW JOLE BLON

Words and Music by
HARRY CHOATES

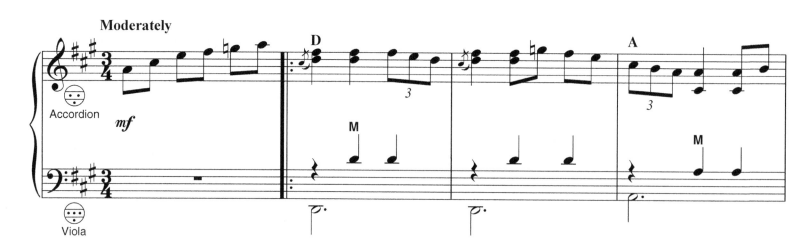

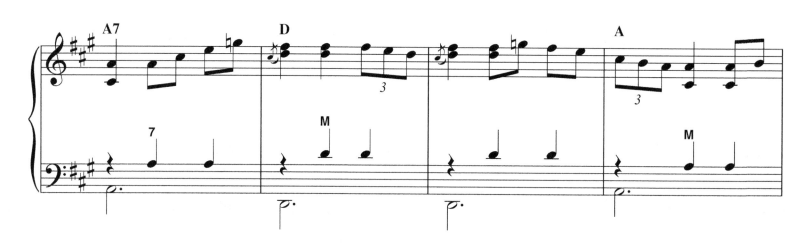